How to
BOOM
B2B SALES

How to
BOOM
B2B SALES

CARMIT YADIN

Archway Publishing books may be ordered through booksellers or by contacting:

Archway Publishing
1663 Liberty Drive
Bloomington, IN 47403
www.archwaypublishing.com
1-(888)-242-5904

Because of the dynamic nature of the Internet, any web addresses or
links contained in this book may have changed since publication and
may no longer be valid. The views expressed in this work are solely those
of the author and do not necessarily reflect the views of the publisher,
and the publisher hereby disclaims any responsibility for them.

Any people depicted in stock imagery provided by Thinkstock are models,
and such images are being used for illustrative purposes only.
Certain stock imagery © Thinkstock.

ISBN: 978-1-4808-1227-7 (sc)
ISBN: 978-1-4808-1229-1 (hc)
ISBN: 978-1-4808-1228-4 (e)

Library of Congress Control Number: 2014918937

Printed in the United States of America.

Archway Publishing rev. date: 01/14/15

ARCHWAY
PUBLISHING

Thank you for reading this book!

Please follow my blog: http://carmityadin.com/.
Get access to outstanding articles about sales,
marketing, and innovation in technology.

Feel free to contact me with any questions or opinions.
I'm always interested in your thoughts and observations.
Please don't hesitate to share them with me!

About the Author

Carmit Yadin is a business leader with a background in various IT industries and experience in communication and building relationships in multicultural environments.

Ms. Yadin is a seasoned expert in many areas of business, and she possesses specialized and proven expertise in business competition management as it relates to the world of technology.

In her blog, she breaks down the ins and outs of the business world so that others can benefit from her wisdom and successes.

Visit Carmit's TEDx Talk –
Why conflicts doesn't have to be distinctive –
https://www.youtube.com/watch?v=N1R84-5DYEA

Contact:
E-mail: Carmit.yadin@gmail.com
LinkedIn: il.linkedin.com/pub/carmit-yadin/4/209/a03/
Twitter: @CarmitYadin

About the Carmit Yadin Blog

Successfully navigating the worlds of business and technology a hundred percent of the time is easier said than done, but if there's anyone who knows how to make it happen, it's Carmit Yadin. Her blog at CarmitYadin.com provides unique and innovative insights, advice, and information for success-oriented individuals looking to reach similar heights in their own careers. Follow Carmit as she blogs and reports on the following:

- Information on how to manage business competition in a variety of areas, such as product marketing, business plan development, international client management, and more.
- Today's hottest technological products and services.
- Tips on how to put your creativity, people skills, and technological background to work for you when it comes to getting ahead in the business world.
- Articles and information on all the latest developments in the world of technology.

Contents

Chapter 1:
Introduction

"I wish I could say it was easy. It wasn't, but it wasn't hard either. But without a strong reason or purpose, anything in life is hard."

—Robert T. Kiyosaki, *Rich Dad, Poor Dad*

This is the first book in the *How to BOOM* series. This guide holds the secret to creating strong sales professionals in the business-to-business (B2B) world. It includes everything you need to know from a sales perspective and everything a sales professional should know in order to make as many sales as possible. The other books in the *How to BOOM* series will address marketing and social media in the B2B world.

The aim of this guide is to help new salespeople in the corporate and B2B worlds, as well as to help existing salespeople improve their skills for better results. It will tell you exactly what you need to know, give you some practice tools and advice, and make B2B sales simple and doable. At the end of each chapter, you will find a helpful summary of what you've just read called *Key Points.* It will give you easy-to-access tools, so you can use it as an ongoing resource during your day-to-day sales tasks.

How this guide came to be

A few years ago, after over a decade in the high-tech industry with experience as an engineer and strong business experience from home, I had my first position in sales. I was very proud of attaining this role in a global company with a global market. I had always wanted to run a sales business on a global scale. It was a great opportunity with huge expectations, both from my superiors and myself.

There was only one thing missing. *I had no experience in actual sales in the B2B market.* I had lots of great skills, but selling wasn't one of them. As soon as I started in sales, I realized it wasn't as easy as I thought it would be.

I watched some very experienced people who were sales leaders and tried to implement their techniques. But as I observed these leaders, I realized that their "old school" techniques weren't working anymore. In this new world and new marketplace, doing the same old things and using the same old techniques just won't work. They won't get you to your goal, and they won't help you win big deals with big corporate companies.

So, with fire in my belly, dedication, tons of mistakes, reading, studying, consulting people I knew, people I didn't, asking every possible question, both right and wrong, spending hours and hours and hours ... I cracked it! I found my way. Now I finally understand the secrets to mastering B2B sales. Now I am a master at anything that has to do with sales. But I will never forget my beginning. Whether someone is just starting out or is a more experienced sales professional looking to improve, I don't want anyone with passion to have to toil as I did. So I wrote this first book in my series.

I believe that if you follow the ideas in this guide and use my experience and knowledge, it will save you tons of time, improve your sales skills, and push you to a new level in B2B sales.

Chapter 2:
What You Need
to Know

"The single most powerful asset we all have is our mind. If it is trained well, it can create enormous wealth in what seems to be an instant."

—Robert T. Kiyosaki, *Rich Dad, Poor Dad*

B 2B (business-to-business) sales are very different from B2C (business-to-consumer). We all have experience in the B2C sales cycle since we have all had a consumer experience, buying everything from computers to pants to homes. This makes B2C sales intuitive and easier for us to understand. B2B is a totally different world, targeting businesses and organizations rather than consumers. Understandably, dealing with an organization is different than dealing with a consumer directly, though at the end of the day it is important to remember we are all communicating with *people*.

B2B sales are when one business supplies products or services to another business. B2B sales are challenging. They involve a long decision-making process, and the sales cycle is quite long as well. As opposed to B2C sales, you will often be dealing with people who know everything about the market, the products you are offering, and other businesses in the market that offer similar products. Therefore, a slight mistake by the company making the sale could send the client running. B2B sales are complicated and need strategic thinking. Many times, you will work with different key people in the same organization. In most cases, you will need to come back a few times until you close the deal.

Clients in B2B sales want the vendor/supplier to put a great deal of value and monetary potential into the deal to prove that the products they will be supplying are of real value. The sales here involve millions—sometimes billions—of dollars. Due to these higher stakes, the decision-making chain is longer and more complicated. There are high volumes of sales involved here. The suppliers must also make sure they will be able to offer the same high volume of product all the time.

B2B salespeople have to remember that their clients know about their business rivals, the kind of products they offer, and the prices they charge. If the supplier makes one wrong step, the client may move to another supplier without another thought. Communication is also important here. If any unavoidable delay occurs, it is important to let the client know in advance. It could mean the difference between losing and retaining a client. Dealing with suppliers that involve billions of dollars is much harder than dealing with individual consumers.

To impress clients, you need to have a great deal of knowledge about the product you are supplying. You need to know it inside out, and you have to remember that you will almost always be dealing with very smart people. The supplier (you) needs to know the benefits, pros, and cons of using the products at hand before attempting to sell them.

B2B sales involve a very complicated process, and every client you find in the market will have different needs. Therefore, you will need to be able to customize your products to fit those needs. With these additional complexities, there are more parties involved in the sales decision. This is unlike a business-to-consumer sale where only two parties are involved. In some cases, business rivals have been forced by circumstances to partner together to meet the needs of the client. While this is good for clients and the supplier's relationships with them, it also causes both suppliers to disclose the way they do business to their rivals, which could lessen the competitive advantage they had previously.

Buyers have many options they can turn to if you do not provide them with what they want. You have to create your sales pitch wisely, to convince them that no project is too hard for you. Before they come to you, they will have studied the market thoroughly. You must have answers to every possible question and a killer sales pitch.

In B2B sales, the challenges are many, and the risks higher because of the big payoff potential. If you are able to meet the needs of your clients, they will keep coming back for more. The same challenges you face are exactly the same challenges other B2B salespeople face. You will need to know the ins and outs of the entire process so it goes smoothly and is clear of as many obstacles as possible. The only similarity between B2B and B2C is that customers' satisfaction comes first. So if it means partnering with your business competitors, so <u>be</u> it.

So, if it's so complicated, why should you put in all this effort? There is one very good reason: the money and the sales volume. B2B sales have huge payoffs; a single large and committed enterprise customer is worth a thousand fickle-minded retail customers. Knowing how to sell B2B is the difference between selling an amazing dish and selling its ingredients. Learning how to master B2B sales won't be a simple task, but actually *doing* it—actually winning the big deal—is one of the best and most invigorating feelings you will ever have.

Key Points

B2B (business-to-business) sales are much more complicated than B2C (business-to-consumer) sales, due to the following:

- In B2B sales, the sales cycle is much longer than the cycle in B2C, as there are many decision makers and more factors are involved.
- The volume of these sales is huge, often involving millions or billions of dollars.
- In B2B sales, the buyers are highly sophisticated, and in most cases they know what they want and what is available in the market. They know about both your company and your competitors.
- Products and services in B2B sales are complicated, and specific knowledge is needed in each area. Understand the specific industry, the specific technology, and be knowledgeable about the product and its benefits. In many cases, you will need to customize your solution to the customer's requirements and work with different parties in his or her company.
- In some cases, you will need to join with one of your business partners to provide a solution.
- In B2B, there are many decision makers involved. Each of them has an opinion, targets, and an agenda. The sales expert must have extraordinary skills and abilities to work on the same deal with different people with a variety of opinions, needs, and agendas.

Chapter 3:
The Keys to B2B Sales

*Manage MB2B sales is to provide big
solutions to big problems.*

Chapter 3:

Before you approach B2B sales, you must understand the concept. B2B sales are different from any sales you have made before. The main aim of B2B sales should be to provide solutions to the problems of other businesses.

Establish a relationship with the client

The best way to approach B2B sales is to create mutually beneficial partnerships with companies and to develop relationships with the decision makers. This will be described in more detail in Chapter 8.

You must create trust between yourself and your customers. If you don't create that trust, you won't sell to them. If you want to do business with your clients for a long time, you need to form and cement a relationship with them. Those relationships will lead them to trust you. That trust will create business. In addition, you need to create a rapport with the company. Be the person whom the manager can trust, someone he or she can call to ask about trends in the market and feel he can consult with.

Closing a deal (especially the first one) with your clients may take longer with these steps, but the rewards will be well worth it, because you will form a long-lasting relationship that will be mutually beneficial for both of you.

Know what your clients want

Your clients know the market very well and they know what they need. However, they are not looking for a salesperson or a supplier *per se*. They are looking for a partner who can help them meet their goals and solve their problems. You must approach

B2B sales with that in mind. You don't just sell a product or service. You sell *solutions* to your customer's problems and needs. It's as simple as that. If what you're offering doesn't relate directly to a problem your customer is facing, you won't be doing business with the company anytime soon. Spend the necessary time to understand your customers' problems and needs. They will pay, listen, and have time for you if you provide them with solutions to their problems.

The buyers

B2B buyers are extremely prepared. In most cases, they already know what you are offering and have planned in advance. They know how your product stands out, and they already know to compare it to your competitors' products. Buyers prepare their orders and purchases in advance based on their needs and problems. Recent research about technology buying behavior suggests that buyers do about 60 percent of the research before they even contact a vendor. About 60 percent of the time, they select their vendor even before the formal selection process begins, and only 20 percent of the time do they decide mid-way through the process. Learn more on buyers and decision makers in Chapter 5.

The solution

You must provide your customer with a total solution and not just approach him or her with a bare-bones description of your product or service. Know all the advantages and disadvantages of the solution you are offering. There are advantages and disadvantages to your product, your customer support, and what your company represents. You must know them all, and you must know how to tell the right story. As a sales professional, you must be ready to inform your customers about the benefits of the solution you are offering them that they can look forward to. On top of that, you must also know the cons, and—more importantly—how to mitigate them and present your total solution in the best way for the client.

In order to do that, you must be well versed in information about the product and must know how the product compares with that of your competitors. A client will want you to give information on how your product will address their problems and, consequently, make a difference in their company.. Be well prepared. Do your research, and know your solution inside and out. You also need to research similar solutions the client could find in the market. For example, if they ask you why they should choose your solution over other solutions in the market, you should know what to tell them. You must know your market. You must know your competitors. You must know your partners, and you must know the industry you are in.

B2B sales life cycle

The B2B sales life cycle is different and longer than that of B2C sales. You must fit the organization requirement, including all organization layers, perform tests (when it's related to technology), get finance approval, and many more layers in the organization that you work for.

There are many processes to be addressed and many tests to be performed. You must be ready for delays, and you may be required to work with more than one decision maker or in different units in the organization. You must fit all the layers of their organization.

In order to keep the life cycle moving, after you complete your first sale, you must continue to invest your resources in your customers. Keep investing your resources and building relationships. Being their expert advisor will make the cycle go round and round, and they will keep buying from you as long as you benefit them. This is the never-ending sales cycle in B2B.

Key Points

- The best way to approach B2B sales is to create mutually beneficial partnerships between companies and develop relationships with the decision makers.
- Know what your clients want. Learn their businesses, and know their problems.
- Don't sell the product or service. Offer a solution to your customers' real problems.
- Be prepared. The buyers already did their homework, and they know the market and your competitors very well.
- Establish a relationship with your client. This is *very important!*
- Know your solution and all of its pros and cons.
- Understand that the sales never end. Know how to keep providing value, keep networking, and keep building relationships with your customers.

Chapter 4:
The Qualities of a Good Sales Professional

"The ability to sell is the number one skill in business. If you cannot sell, don't bother thinking about becoming a business owner."

—Robert T. Kiyosaki, *Rich Dad, Poor Dad*

Yes, relationships are one of the keys to success in B2B sales. But are they enough? Definitely not! It's a given that sales professionals must be nice. You may think that's one of the keys to success in sales, but not when it comes to B2B sales! In B2B, the risks and demands are very high, and the customers are extremely sophisticated. Being nice is not enough. Nice is nice, but in this industry it doesn't deliver. In the business-to-business world it takes a lot to win, and even more to succeed. All those *nice* guys must push themselves and their customers out of their respective comfort zones and focus on delivering value. (For more on this, see Chapter 7.)

So, what does it take from the salesperson?

*What qualities do we need to adopt
in order to sell successfully?*

The perfect relationship with the client

Creating a working rapport and lasting relationships are definitely key. However, that is only part of the bigger picture, and no—it is not even close to enough. You have to be nice, courteous, and you must be a proactive communicator, sending and answering e-mails promptly; but even that is not enough. The stakes are very high in B2B sales. The finances involved in this project can be very high. It will take much more than courtesy and being proactive. Look at it this way: making the sale and getting the client is a puzzle. Forming good relationships will contribute one piece of your success to that puzzle.

You must have the ability and knowledge to build the *right* relationship with the customer. The tricky part is that you must know how to work in different environments and how to build trust with different people and different organizations. Another issue here is that in many cases B2B business involves different cultures and different countries. The sales professional must be eager and prepared to build relationships in multicultural environments.

A hard worker who goes the extra mile

You must be ready to work harder than everyone else at your company. You must be ready for long and impromptu meetings with your clients. If you are required to, travel to them to get closer to closing that deal. Always be there when your clients and your organization need you. Everyone likes to deal with a person who is always there, standing by whenever he or she is needed. You can't compromise. Do everything it takes in order to close the deal in the best way you can for all parties.

Understand your clients inside and out

You must know the challenges they face in their business and the competition in their market. Basically, know how their business runs. You must always see things from the perspective of the client.

A problem solver

Whenever issues arise, the right salesperson will address them as quickly as possible and give the customer the feeling that he or she is in control and that everything is going as smoothly as possible.

Be a one-man show *and* a team player

In most cases, the salesperson is out in the field alone and must represent the company in the best way possible. On top of that, he or she must also work well within the company and with the team. Therefore, the salesperson must know how to handle both situations: being a one-man show in the field and being with the customer, as well as being a good team player internally with the manager and coworkers.

Understand the dynamics in the market

You need to understand how the market trends change so you can prepare appropriate messages suitable to different situations. Every client is unique, and even though your solution can work for all of them, you need to tailor your message in a way that shows the quantifiable results they will gain with your business. You must understand the market and their needs. You must know how to solve your customers' constantly changing problems.

With the above skills and new approach, customers will need you, their salesperson, and will seek you out. Great sales professionals provide value to their customers through a three-pillar approach of *teaching, tailoring,* and *taking control.*

The salesperson's ability to *teach* their customers or challenge their thinking, to give them information and ideas to be more competitive, and to save money or generate new income—these all matter to the customer. Through an understanding of the economic drivers in the customer's industry, sales professionals must *tailor* their sales messages to address the specific quantifiable results each customer is looking for. Know everything you can about the field and the company, and you can *take control* of the sale. Create a different speech, a different way of thinking for each customer. Be unique, loyal, and indispensable to your customers and the company you work for, and without a doubt, you will start closing more great sales.

Key Points

- Create a rapport and a lasting relationship with your client. Build trust with people in the organizations. This can be difficult, but work for this even in multicultural environments.
- Work extra hard, and go the extra mile. Be ready to meet your customers' needs. Be available to your clients and to the company when they need you.
- Understand your clients' needs and challenges, and how their businesses operate.
- Take control of the sale. Should any issue arise, be ahead of it and resolve it quickly.
- Understand the market in which you are operating in terms of trends. Be ready to go out of your way to customize the solution to fit the needs of each client.
- Be able to work well alone in the field, with the customer, *and* as a team player at the office with coworkers.
- Be ready to train and teach clients how to use the various aspects of the solution.
- Be willing to challenge the customers. Push them out of their comfort zone. Help them see challenges that could crop up in the future, and show them how your solution could take care of them.

Chapter 5:
Understand the
Decision Makers

The focus is their *financial result, not yours.*

B efore reaching out to decision makers you must understand their world and their way of thinking. Understanding them, their needs, and how the company environment affects them will help you ask the right questions and present your solution in the best way.

The most important thing to know about decision makers is that these people are under intense and constant pressure to deliver strong financial results to their shareholders. The board members and shareholders are pushing them and expect outstanding financial results every quarter. The stock price is unforgiving, and those results are crucial for the company and their own positions. With that pressure comes constant action. They are always busy and always working to maximize their profitability and increase company revenues. All this means that they will prefer to invest their money where they will have strong ROI (return on investment). They will expect a quick turnaround for ROI as well. The people you speak with are overwhelmed with all the work they have, and every new fire that pops up brings them new tasks, making it even harder to catch up. They must prioritize and focus only on the most important things.

More than ever, companies are focusing on their core business, what they know how to do best, and outsourcing their other activities. We used to think that technology improves our lives, but when it comes to decision makers, it makes their lives harder. Sometimes technology actually makes it impossible to stay on top of their work. There are too many e-mails a day, too many items on the *to do* and *must do today* lists. They are bombarded with marketing messages from companies they know want to sell them something. You can be sure they already know not only your product and your company, but also your competitors and their prices.

Decision makers have their own agendas within their organizations, and they always want to improve their positions. They want to please their boss, and if their decision to buy your product displeases the boss, they could have a serious problem. They don't have time to deal with future problems; they have too many current ones on their plates. Do your homework. Knowing all the potential outcomes and results of their purchasing from you can help assuage those concerns and close the sale for you.

Decision makers don't want to improve a system that works! Especially if there is no immediate ROI; mostly they will see it as a waste of time and money. Their main focus is *their* financial result, not yours.

And remember, decision makers are just human beings. Just like you and me, they weren't designed to have so many problems on their minds that they don't sleep at night. What they are looking for are solutions. Give them a real solution to their problems and they will listen to you. They will cooperate with you, and they will buy from you.

Key Points

- Decision makers are busy people. Keep your conversations focused and to the point.
- Remember that your customers are under pressure for good financial results by the stockholders.
- They are informed about your products and even about competitors' products.
- Understand that the clients have a lot on their plates. Buying your product may not be on their priority list, especially if it does not increase the company's profits.
- Offer your clients solutions to their problems so they will listen to you and buy from you.
- Decision makers are focused on their company's profits, not yours. They intend to invest their money where there are higher returns to maximize their profits. Have an understanding of how their company works and what they need so you can help them make the best decision.

Chapter 6:
What You Really
Need to Ask

"Ask the right questions if you're **going
to find the right answers."**

- Vanessa Redgrave

T o sell to your customers, you need to ask the right questions. In order to sell, you must understand why your customers would buy from you. If you don't understand your customers, you won't be able to sell to them. Understanding the reasons customers are buying will boost your sales like magic. If you understand them, they will return your calls, agree to pay more, and won't compare prices.

Customers will buy because

1. they enjoy working with you as a salesperson, especially when you create personal relationships with them. In B2B sales, relationships are very important (See Chapter 8.);

2. they believe and trust you; you are honest as their salesperson;

3. they know you are always there for them whenever they need you;

4. they understand why they need your products and how they benefit their businesses;

5. they understand how the products they are buying will improve their businesses. They understand your products; and

6. You offer a fair price. This will be the icing on the cake, and not necessarily the main determining factor. Most customers are ready to pay any price if you can show them the value your products or services can add to their businesses. (You can read more on this in Chapter 12.)

If you follow these six guidelines, your customers will know that your focus is on them, and they will buy from you.

What to ask the customer

As a professional you should make an effort to understand your customers' businesses. If you know their businesses and fields of competition well, you can anticipate the kinds of questions they are likely to ask you. Likewise, you can know the right questions to ask them.

Here are a few questions you can ask your potential or existing customers:

1. What is your budget for this project?
2. What are your company's values—corporate as well as individual?
3. What do you feel excited about for the next twelve months, and what are you looking forward to for your company?
4. How has your company done/managed without these products or services in the past?
5. What kinds of risks do you face when you deal with inevitable changes?
6. What are your business goals for the coming months, and how do you plan to use our products to achieve those goals?
7. *If it is a return customer, you need to ask a question in the form of a follow up.* For example: How is our product doing? How do you find it?
8. If we do this for you, will you adopt our product?

There are so many questions that a salesperson can ask. However, when you feel that you are near closing the sale, you can ask the final crucial question: "Who will make the last decision? Can I speak to him or her?"

The most important thing is to ask the *right* questions and then listen to the answers without interrupting. Good sales professionals listen actively. They give their undivided attention to the potential customer as they speak. They also ask questions about the short and long-term goals of a company, so customers can know if their products and services can help them achieve their companies' goals.

Key Points

- Customers buy because:
  - They have a great relationship with you, and they trust you.
  - They enjoy working with you. You provide them with great support and fast response times.
  - They understand why they need your products and how they benefit their businesses.
  - You offer a fair price.
- Understand the customer's business. You can do this by asking the right questions about the long and short-term goals of the business.
- Listen to your customer's answers without interrupting. This is the only way to get to know if your products will help the business meet your customer's goals.

Chapter 7:
Understand Your Customer's Needs

You have to see the world through their eyes.

In this world of options and information, customers have become smarter and tougher. They have less available time, and they expect you to accommodate them. Understanding this—and catering specifically to targeted customers—is one of the main requirements leading companies have for a vendor.

With the open market, and information about products and services easily discoverable, customers will no longer be coming to you blind. They will have done their research. They will know prices and all the details they need to know. Unless you put yourself in their place, walk in their shoes, and see the market from their perspective, you will never make any headway with them. B2B sales professionals must know their customers as thoroughly as possible.

You must know the *company.* This includes the market, what customers are going after, and who their competitors are. A sales professional who understands what the customer needs and who approaches the sale from a business point of view will know what to offer and how to become indispensable to the customer. Know your customer's wishes and problems so you will be able to provide the necessary information and the best solution.

Understand your customers from their personal and political points of view. They want to say the right things to the right people; more goes on at their companies than you know. Understand the internal balance of power, and be loyal to the decision makers you work with.

Three things to consider

1. Business-to-business sales should focus on selling a solution. It is challenging to sell a solution when you do not know what the customer needs. Bonding with customers is the only way you will be able to cater to their needs. Customer satisfaction is crucial. It helps build loyalty and is the biggest differentiator of success and failure in all business segments. The key is to understand the needs of your customers.

2. Customers want to be understood. They want a seller who tries to solve their needs rather than one who tries to sell them a product. Customers want to build relationships. If they do not like the salesperson, they will never buy.

3. Customers are the business's lifeline, and to keep your business thriving, you need to give your time and understand their needs. One of the best secrets of sales is keeping the client at the heart of your business. Make them feel like the most essential component in the transaction. The only way you will ever achieve this is through understanding their needs.

Communicate with your customer

Customers are the crucial element of a business. The ability to reach out and relate to them requires a fundamental and powerful tool: communication. The goal is to make the customer feel valued. Communication identifies possible problems and issues, and it helps you find out new and emerging requirements that may be very helpful in the future.

Always initiate a conversation with your customers. Ask questions and learn from their responses whether they are satisfied with the service you are offering or if they are experiencing any problems. From consistent communication with your customers, you can learn how they think. Thus, you can tell them exactly what they want to hear. They want to hear that you have a solution for them, and that your products are a notch higher in value than what your rivals offer.

Be a good listener, too. This encourages openness to suggestions that could help you conduct your business. If a customer has a complaint, it only means he or she is concerned. It is important to take it as a challenge and strive to improve your product and company. One of the best ways to understand the needs of your customers is to pay extra attention and make a change when they make negative remarks. Negative feedback is an indication that you are not fulfilling their needs, so pay attention and strive for a better experience for them. Interact with your customers regularly to improve the relationship you share.

Know who the right contact is for you and who makes the decisions. You can't talk to everyone at the company. Find your contacts. It's important to have your own contacts, because once you get through to them you will be able to supply whatever they need. In many cases, a lot of petty politics happen within the company. If you know the politics, you will know how to swing them in your favor. That is very important. Know what goes on in the boardroom—or at least get a hint—and you will know how to play your cards.

Know your contact personally

Know your contact really well.

It is important to do business directly with your customers, because it tells you exactly what the customers need. Being knowledgeable helps during the promotion of your products and services. Ensure that your customer's representatives are professionals and knowledgeable, and know the right way to respond to inquiries made by the customer.

One thing customers appreciate is a business with alternatives and options. This makes them feel that the business has their best interest at heart because they are flexible and working for them. This is a technique that makes them feel that they are a crucial part of your business and that they are getting special treatment. If you make customers your business friends, you will easily understand their needs for business-to-business sales.

The personal point of view was mentioned in Chapter 5, but it bears repeating here. You must know the decision makers from a personal point of view. Know something about their personal lives. This is very tricky and really depends on the prospective decision maker. As we know, business is between *people*. We all must get to know the person in front of us and with time build personal trust and share personal information. A relationship with the individual who might buy your products is essential. Don't miss this absolutely critical step!

Thoroughly knowing and understanding the customers and delivering what they want is the ultimate key to success. Whether sales are increasing, flat, or declining, we should spend quality time with our buyers to understand what's on their minds and respond appropriately. The decisions customers make will be based on how they trust their suppliers and the people they work with. The above three ways to know your customers will make you stand out as professional and desired by your customers.

Key Points

- Understand the customers. Know the market and competitors. This is how you will know which products to sell them.
- Maintain friendly relationships with your customers. Know the decision makers personally to improve your relationship.
- Know the balance of power in your customers' companies. Be loyal to the decision maker in the organizations.
- Find out if your customers are satisfied with your products and if the products are addressing the problems adequately.
- Be a good listener so customers can share with you. They should feel comfortable telling you even the negatives of your products.

Chapter 8:
Stop Selling to
BOOM Your Sales

Business is between people, not companies.

I n order to close more sales, you must stop selling. Yes, that's correct!

To increase your sales and revenues you must stop selling, and put your efforts into *building relationships*. These relationships will create endless sales cycles for you. The main reason for that is that people will buy from someone who

- understands what they want;
- understands what they need;
- can fulfill their need;
- they can trust;
- educates them;
- provides them with relevant information;
- solves their problem;
- creates opportunities for them; and
- provides them with great value on their product.

Building relationships is all about values and trust. Put your energy into understanding your customers' values. Provide them with good value financially. Always be honest and tell the truth. Make them need you. Make them want to consult you when they have issues to solve, and then help them solve those problems. Be their expert advisor.

Relationships are crucial to business-to-business sales. They are what keep the business operational. Relationships establish great connections and bring more business opportunities. They also drive business, since people believe in you and see how you could satisfy their needs. Relationships are not a one-time thing; they cannot be built overnight but are developed over time.

In the business world there are not specific methodologies. Every case, every customer, and every partner—each one of them is in a totally different world, and that's the beauty of this business. Good business isn't static, and there isn't a hard and fast system of dos and don'ts. Each case is special.

This is very different from the traditional sales strategies proffered by sales gurus twenty or thirty years ago. Often, the advice they gave was about overcoming fears of cold calling, combined with outdated sales techniques. Those strategies just aren't nearly as effective as they once were.

If you want to create revenue, increase customer satisfaction, and drive brand equity, stop selling and start adding value.

The sale is not about you, your company, your products, or your services. It's about your customer. Only when you understand this will you be able to rapidly increase your sales. Business is done between people, not between companies. Again, relationships will make your business thrive. It's the key to making sales and offers come to you.

The world we live in is hooked on technology. We connect virtually more than we socialize face-to-face. As our social lives become more and more virtual, I find that building relationships, face-to-face interaction, and that special human touch are very important. We are all human, and although we appreciate technology, we want to really connect with people in the flesh. But this connection, this human touch, is becoming more and more rare. One of my favorite movies, *Up in the Air*, has a great example that emphasizes the importance and value of face-to-face meetings. When Natalie Keener (Anna Kendrick) An ambitious, freshly graduated was just hired to Career Transitions Corporation (CTC) a company that informing workers of their dismissals in place of their employers, who fear doing it themselves.

Natalie promote a plan to cut costs by conducting layoffs via <u>videoconferencing</u>. Ryan Bingham (<u>George Clooney</u>) who build his life around flying frequently argues that Natalie knows nothing on the actual process and that cant be done remotely it has to be face to face.

There were problems while implementing this new program while one man breaks down in tears before the camera, while Natalie was unable to comfort him. The other big problem that cause the company to put this program on hold was when a woman that was fired killed herself by jumping from a bridge, as she said she would,

The idea behind this movie is that there is no replacement for a face to face meeting and the personal touch. The way I see it the human touch has strong influence in making business and that cant be replace by any technology or any different way of communication.

My recommendation is that you will put your resources on the human dimension, put attention on the personal aspects. Go meet your customers, partners, competitors and build relationships with them.

A human, personal touch and face-to-face meetings are crucial to increase sales and keep your business running.

Building relationships is essential to your business, but they must be quality relationships, based on in-person meetings (if possible) and a personal, individual, and human touch.

Key Points

- Stop selling.
- Make sure you build relationships with the right contacts in the organization.
- It's all about values. Provide your customers with real values, and they're yours.
- Stop selling and start listening to your customers' requirements and needs.
- Throw away the sales pitch and start a real conversation.
- Always tell the truth. Cherish your honesty as one of your greatest assets.
- Understand what your customers really want. Ask questions. Ask the reason for purchasing your solution. Start with an open, conversational approach. Talk about a certain issue that your product or services can solve.
- Keep the human touch. Meet with your customers and really talk to them.
- Remember, relationships are crucial to your business, but they aren't all of it.

Chapter 9:
How to Build Trust

"Profit comes as a result of being good at what you do.
Trust comes as a result of being good at why you do it."

—Simon Sinek

Trust is a core concept in business and plays a major role in building relationships. Business-to-business sales need trust, which doesn't happen overnight.

A customer will never allow a person he or she does not trust into his or her business. Selling is being able to convince, persuade, and win a customer, thus building a strong bond of trust. Being able to make customers trust you and the products or services you offer is the best way to be successful. If you can build trust, you can make the sale.

Important B2B relationships are not just with your customers. Build relationships with your vendors, business partners, and even with your competitors. It is impossible to run a business without these relationships. They will carry you through challenging times in your business.

Trust Creation Process

The perfect process for building trust in business-to-business sales is right here.

- *Engage*: The way to get attention from a customer is through communication, but to create trust you need to have an open discussion. Engaging a customer is key.
- *Listen*: Pay attention. There is nothing more frustrating than talking to someone who seems uninterested. This is a huge turnoff to a potential client. Listen carefully and offer solutions when needed.

- *Timing*: Learn to find the right time to frame the core issue. Show customers that you care and that they can trust you.
- *Foresight*: Look ahead and try to predict problems and solutions. Be clear in all conversations.
- *Commit*: Actions speak louder than words. Show actions of commitment and you earn trust.

The fact of the matter is that business relationships are like any other relationship. They are based on trust between people. No one will buy from someone they don't like, and they certainly won't trust them. These relationships must be mutually beneficial. Make an effort to maintain this trust.

How to build trust

Building trust is not easy, but it must be done because it is ultimately what will drive B2B sales. You will be required to make some effort. Building relationships is not a one-off, but rather a process that takes time, progressing from one step to another. Just building the relationship is not enough. You will have to sustain it, too. You must seek day-to-day interactions with customers to maintain the trust you have built. Should this trust erode, you will lose sales.

Here are a few rules for you to follow:

- *Honesty* – This is the most important of all the rules. If you are honest, you will easily earn the trust of others. Trust will come if you can approach selling as helping the customer find a solution to a problem. You need to know what the customer needs, and if you feel that your product or service cannot fit that exactly, you should not be afraid to tell the customer that your product may not meet all of his or her needs.

- *Reliability* – Always be there, all the time. Let the customers know (from your actions) that they can always count on you to be there.
- *Walk away from a sales situation* – No one likes salesmen! Even when they really need the product that you are selling, no one likes to listen to a sales pitch. When meeting your customers, you need to act and speak as if you have met your colleague or friend.
- *Give them deals* – For customers to build a relationship with you, they will be looking for value from you. Can you offer them that? If so, you will sustain the relationship.
- *Have a real dialogue* – Every time you meet with a customer, you should turn that meeting into a dialogue. Think of it as a chat with a colleague or friend. Be an active listener and, no matter what, avoid making a sales pitch. Make sure you chat about business, not personal things or idle chitchat.
- *Be professional* – Professionalism means that you are serious about what you do and what you offer. Customers tend to trust people who take time to understand what they do. You should learn as much as possible about your customer's business.
- *Show real integrity* – Always stand by what you know is right, no matter what your company or the customer may think. If it means taking a stand that will not be popular with your customers, take it and stick by it.

Building a relationship and gaining the trust of a customer is paramount, but as I've stated before, it is only part of the bigger picture of making B2B sales. Gaining that trust is the first component to seek, because if customers don't trust you, they will buy from someone else.

Key Points

- Know that trust is crucial in sales, since customers buy from people they trust.
- Build trust through engaging, listening, sharing your vision, and committing to the customer. This takes time and effort, like in all other relationships.
- A loss of trust can lead to loss of sales.
- Remember and pay attention to the five rules in this chapter in order to build trust.
  - Honesty
  - Reliability
  - Offering value and having a dialogue (not a sales pitch)
  - Being professional
  - Showing integrity

Chapter 10:
Create Your Sales
Message

*"The more I risk being rejected, the better
my chances are of being accepted."*

Robert T. Kiyosaki, *Rich Dad, Poor Dad*

C reating the right sales message is one of the first ways to get "in" with your customers. The sales message acts as the prospectus of your business, providing information to potential customers. A good sales message should offer a story prospects can't refuse.

Create an attention-seeking headline

It is important to create an enticing message with the power to capture a client's attention. This will make them curious to read more. To come up with the best headline, ask yourself what the targeted group is. Whom do you want to read it? Asking yourself this question can get you started down the right path.

Use believable claims

When you create a message to entice customers, make sure to be correct, authentic, and honest. When claims sound too good to be true, the potential customer will assume they *are*. Do not exaggerate. It will chase customers away.

Genuine testimonials

If you want to build trust with your prospects, then you need to include authentic testimonials. It is through the testimonials of past customers that you can prove that your business will work for prospective clients.

Testimonials can help outweigh the skepticism of a prospective customer. To have genuine testimonials, always ask for them from your clients and customers. Ask permission to use real names and addresses; anonymous testimonials are not easily believed.

Give them special offers

In business, offers are important. Having an offer in your advertisement is likely to attract more customers than a flat advertisement. Conduct research to find out what the market really needs, and use that knowledge to create an offer. The way to attract people is by hitting on areas that affect their day-to-day lives. Including a hard-to-resist offer in every sales message is a powerful tip to increase your number of responses.

Make a risk-free transaction

You may hear of a person who needs something but isn't buying it. You wonder why. The answer is that people are always afraid of purchasing something they fear may not be exactly what they need. When it comes to B2B sales, one wrong move can have serious repercussions. In your sales message, ensure the customer's satisfaction. It is important to include a money back guarantee or an additional offer, like continued services with no additional charge. With risk-free transactions, potential customers are more likely to buy.

Create an enthralling conclusion

A majority of prospects have a tendency to read the headline, a bit of introduction, and then jump to the conclusion. When creating a sales message, take advantage of this. Make sure that you conclude with something that will stimulate their interest. Emphasize the important things and benefits offered, and spark their interest so they read the entire message.

Give the prospective client a compelling reason

With all the above said and done, give prospective clients a compelling reason as to why they should buy your product. Create a sales message that offers incentives for making a sale right away. Remember, B2B sales are different from B2C. B2B customers are more informed, know prices, and know your rivals. Therefore, you want to tell them about the value of your products and services. What will they gain with *your* products versus those of your competitors?

Key Points

- Use genuine testimonials from past customers with real names and addresses. (Ask permission first!)
- Give special offers in your sales message.
- Provide risk-free transactions by giving money-back guarantees and continuous service with no additional charge.
- Your conclusion should pique the customer's interest and make him or her want to read the entire sales message.
- Offer the customer every possible reason to buy your products by telling him or her their assets and values.

Chapter 11:
Fire Up Your
Sales Meeting

"Most people think *selling* is the same as *talking*.
But the most effective salespeople know that
listening is the most important part of their job."

—Roy Bartell

As discussed earlier, decision makers have limited time, so when they set up a meeting with you, you must make the most of it. In order to do that, the sales professional must efficiently lead the meeting.

It is his or her responsibility to ensure that the meeting runs efficiently without wasting time. The meeting should be well organized with a set agenda so you do not end up with confusion, angry clients, or—worse yet—a meeting in which you didn't achieve your goals.

Use the following guidelines to make your meetings more efficient.

Know the client

For you to have a successful meeting, you must know your client. This will help when you are in the meeting or making a sales pitch. You must learn their needs in advance, and know how your solution can help them. Do your research and look for information about the clients from their Web sites, and ask people who work with them, such as your business partners. You can also make calls to the organization to find out more information.

Set and distribute the agenda before the meeting takes place

Having an agenda will ensure that the meeting runs smoothly. All the parties know what is going to transpire in the meeting, preventing any stumbling blocks. Make sure you have created an agenda and distributed it to the clients before the day of the meeting. This will help the clients prepare for the meeting. It is also helpful in ensuring that there is natural flow of communication, since all the parties are aware of what is to be discussed.

Decide on the venue

For most clients, you will end up meeting in their offices. If that is not the case, you should look for a quiet venue that is convenient for the client and for you.

Bring your marketing tools

Always arrive at meetings armed with your tools. This includes samples, brochures, and writing materials.

Ensure that everyone is participating in the meeting

Sending a meeting confirmation twenty-four hours before the meeting is crucial. It will ensure that the meeting will, in fact, take place and all participants will be there. During the meeting, everyone should participate so that the meeting can be productive. It is your role to ensure that the participants are given equal time to air their views and to ask questions. This will allow the meeting to be productive and for knowledge to be shared.

Turn conflicts into ideas

It is common to have conflicts in meetings since people often have different opinions on a subject. It is your responsibility to transform these conflicts into healthy arguments, which may lead to better understanding of issues. Your role is to ensure that the conflicts do not rise above polite disagreements. You should be in control of the meeting in such a way that you can redirect any aggression. The conflict should be used to find solutions instead of creating a wedge.

Make sure you are listening to your customers and that you understand their needs. Make sure you can provide top-of-the-line solutions to their problems with great values.

Follow up

Just like with any other sales activity, you have to follow up on the meeting and on the action items. The follow-up responsibility is on you. Don't wait for others. After the meeting, send the meeting summary to all the attendees and include the open action items. Your responsibility is to keep a close eye on the process.

Key Points

- Find out information about your client.
- Set the agenda for the meeting.
- Determine the venue of the meeting.
- Bring your marketing tools.
- Make sure that everyone participates in the meeting.
- Manage conflicts to turn them into ideas.
- Follow up!

Chapter 12:
Break Your Pitch
Into Small Bites

"The word impossible is not in my dictionary."

—Napoleon Bonaparte

It is every B2B salesperson's dream to get business from the big corporate companies. After all, selling to a big company means more sales and more money. Making that dream a reality is the difficult part. Selling to a large company is tough and intimidating. You may wonder where to start, and even whether such a large company could possibly be interested in doing business with you. It all feels a little impossible.

So how you can take on that impossible
task and boom your sales?

Understand that it *is* possible. You can do it. You just have to make it *simple*. Simplicity is the key to any seemingly impossible task. The way to create that simplicity is to break down your big target into small tasks.

Don't approach the corporation. Approach the unit.

Every company has its own organizational structure; corporations are divided into smaller business units. Remembering this fact will help you approach your task efficiently. By this, I mean the following: aim for the company in its entirety, but approach its smaller units. This will make it easy for you to penetrate the organization without being intimidated by its size. Target a branch of the company. This will allow you to get to know the decision makers in that branch and also discover more information about the branch. With that, it will be easier to implement your campaign and get yourself in the door. Another option is to approach one of the R&D units or the IT department. Look for the right *in* for you and your product.

Go in with an easy yes

Don't overwhelm them and yourself by offering all your products right away. Offer them the easiest solution, something they need *now*, and something they will say *yes* to. Approach the company offering only the products that solve an overlooked issue in their business. This will give you an opportunity to show your worth to the company, and it creates an opportunity to get more orders for other products in the future. It is much easier for you to increase an existing business from this starting point.

Be prepared

Don't just show up. You have to be prepared. (Don't forget to read Chapter 11.) If you want to talk to the decision makers, you need to have information about the company at your fingertips. This will prevent wasting time, since they won't have to explain what their business is all about. Their schedules are full. You need to fit yourself into their schedules. You can do this by arming yourself with information about the company and how your products can work for them. Make it easy and worth their while for them to meet with you.

Focus on their potential benefits

The company you are targeting needs to know the benefits your products will offer. Focus your sales pitch on that, instead of talking about what your products are and your goals. For instance, the decision makers may want to know how the product may reduce processing time. Have a complete and thorough answer for them, and explain how the product will work for *them*—not how it will work for you.

Chapter 12:

Don't give up too easily

For B2B sales, patience and persistence are important. Don't throw in the towel just because your six attempts to contact the decision maker haven't yielded results. This is especially true for top-level executives who are busy all the time. Make up to twelve contact attempts before you decide to give up.

Look out for events that can trigger changes in the company

Events like mergers, new leadership, and economic issues can present opportunities for you to make your entry into the organization.

Establish relationships with different people in the organization

This will safeguard you in case there is a change of command in the organization. Establish contact with all the people concerned with your account, since most decisions in the company will involve many people.

Key Points

- Approach the smaller unit.
- Go in with your best and simplest offering.
- Be prepared. Research the company before making your first contact.
- Present the benefits of your products to the company.
- Be persistent.
- Take advantage of trigger events to penetrate a company.
- Establish relationships with different people who are in decision-making positions in the company.

Chapter 13:
Networking in
B2B Sales

Your contacts will make or break your success.

B usiness networking is the best tool you have to build your relationships and boom your sales. The right contacts can help you attain your targets, give you credibility, and bring you success, so whether your business is small or large, a strong network will help it grow and succeed.

Networking leverages business connections, bringing more connections to your business and you to them. The best business relationships are based on sharing valuable information that leads to opportunities and ideas, as well as providing a useful support system.

Networking requires more than knowing some businesses, shaking a bunch of hands, having a drawer full of business cards, or attending networking functions and events. It's good to make friends and socialize, but there is much more to it when your goal is increasing your business. Your business network relies on mutually beneficial relationships between people; other people will only want to network with you when they know you can help them in some way.

The importance of networking in business-to-business sales

Networking is a crucial concept in B2B sales. Every activity carried out from one business to another is aided by a strong network. It helps in business planning and poaching, helps develop sales leads, and teaches you how to conduct and direct your business well. Your network contains a depth of potential contacts. The most critical component to a business is creating the awareness about your existence, and your network can spread the word. The focus of business networking should be building strong relationships. Learn to stop making sales first and instead start to connect and build the right network.

Of course, sales will follow later, but the most important thing is laying a good foundation and cornerstone of your business. This is done by establishing relationships that can grow to offer new opportunities in the future. These new opportunities in the market are essential; they help you meet even more businesses and individuals who will help you expand your business network.

Business networking

In order to be efficient, you must have an idea of whom you would like to know—your targets. Make some lists. You should have a list of sales targets, including customers and partners you'd like to work with. If you have your target list, you can determine the people you should—or *want*—to know.

Once you have identified key contacts, figure out where you will find them to have an opportunity to interact with them. There are three things to consider:

1. Think about people you know who are connected to your target.

2. Think about the people you expect to meet at the next event you are going to. Go to the events your customers will be attending.

3. Use social media to learn about your targeted list. Give each person detail in your mind and see them as more than a number. It will be easier for you to connect with them and will more easily lead to a meeting.

It's important to understand that having tons of business cards and lots of contacts won't help you. While those may seem impressive, in reality it's better to be focused on your target list. It's about *quality* not quantity. Having one or two contacts who are actually helpful is much more valuable than having the business cards of fifty people who will barely remember your face.

Now you have to prepare for your meetings. First impressions are important. Do your homework to learn as much as possible about the individual, his or her business, and any important business issues. Make sure you've taken the time to prepare an introduction of yourself and your business, as well as prepared some great questions and conversations to engage your networking prospect. During your meeting you can talk about anything, but in the back of your mind remember what you're selling and what you're working for.

How to increase networking in B2B sales

When you need to increase sales, you should know the right businesses to network with and where to network. You should be in a position to select the right field and the right event at which to interact with the best target.

The first step is determining which contact in your list is most worth meeting. You should do this before thinking of adding networking functions to your schedule or considering another strategy of networking. After identifying this contact, figure out how to meet him or her. Keep in mind that you are not the only business looking to expand its network. To stand out, be impeccable. Everything you do should be carefully considered. You can't afford missteps.

Prepare for your top prospect meeting carefully. Remember that the first impression is crucial. You may not get a chance to change their minds. Make conversation, have good timing with the introduction and question session, and engage with your networking prospect. Keep it quick, but not clipped. Let your prospect talk and listen, and you will understand what you can offer and what the prospect is looking for. After the meeting, it's incredibly important to follow up. My advice is to strike while the iron is hot; don't wait more than a week to follow up with your prospects.

Each business relationship must be judged independently to know what step to take next. If you discussed business during your first interaction and said you would follow up to schedule a meeting, a call and/or follow up e-mail are appropriate. If you sent an initial e-mail or note and don't hear back, you may want to place a call or send another e-mail, perhaps with some industry news that is relevant to what you discussed. But don't persist to the point of being annoying. You want to stay in touch, but you don't want to irritate them.

Key Points

- Make a list of the people you would like to meet.
- Learn who can help you reach your goals; make a list.
- Find out who can introduce you to those people.
- Learn about your target; go for details.
- Go to the events they are attending.
- Be prepared for your meetings by researching the target and his or her business.
- Have a great conversation.
- Follow up on the meeting promptly.
- Give them a good value, so they will continue needing you.

Chapter 14:
It's Not About Price

"The more value you provide, the less price matters."

- Jeffrey Gitomer

The two main targets for any company are sales growth and profit growth. This is how companies are measured these days, both by themselves and externally. This is the information they present to the world and to their investors. The sale price is integral to staying on top of those numbers, both to you as a sales professional and to management.

In B2B, the companies you work with and your customers will push you for price reduction. This isn't because they just want to argue the price with you. It's because the sale is complicated, and there are a lot of factors at work on their side of the deal. There are many things to discuss and review, not to mention that there are a bunch of competitors out there.

So, how can you win the deal without going into a price war?
How you can sell without compromising on the price?
Is it right or wrong to be expensive?

The good news is: there is a way! Selling on value. People are willing to pay more for a product they think will give them a truly special experience or a significant value—if you present it to them in the right way.

Selling on value, not price, involves a balance of confidence, personal rapport, and doing your homework. It has become more difficult, since buyers are smart and have resources to explore the market and get to know it well.

Value is based on the products (or services) provided offering better solutions than those of competitors. This often includes meeting additional needs the customer did not even realize existed.

The challenge is communicating that value to the customer. Once the value is outlined, the customer should be willing to pay.

Setting the price using value-based pricing is beneficial to your business. A business can set a high price depending on the benefits offered to the customer. It should always offer the best possible product to its customers. It should ensure that the products solve the customer's problems, and exceed expectations. This gives the business an opportunity to set its products and services apart from the competition. If the customer can value your product more than the competitor's, he is ready to pay for it. Customers are ready to pay for solutions they cannot find elsewhere—solutions that address all their immediate and potential concerns. Your business should focus on providing solutions of the best value.

So, what is the product's value, really?
How do you keep the price high and still make the sale?
How do you use value to sell and improve
your business relationships?

The first thing to know about value is that you have to lead with it. You must present it up front before you get into the price discussion. Present it to everyone you think will need your product, and do so often.

See the value from your customer's point of view. Your customers will pay more for:

- Brand names: Take Cisco, for example. Cisco's prices are higher, yet IT managers keep choosing Cisco over the competition.
- Customer service: Customer service is the key to creating loyal customers. Customers will pay more for a thorough, personal, pleasant, and professional experience with customer service.

- The salesperson: When the salesperson is committed to his or her customer's needs and their relationship—and is loyal and accessible—customers trust and value him or her.
- Financial values: In general, it's easier to make a sale if you can present the customer a speedy ROI and details as to how the product supports business growth. If your product will support your customer's business growth with fast ROI, it will improve your chances of winning the sale. This turns the tables and makes buying from you a source of income for them, not an expense. Present it that way.
- Product values:
  - Simplicity: Make it simple to implement and manage.
  - Features: More, better, and more useful features.
  - High quality.
  - Integration: The product can integrate easily into the customer's existing infrastructure and available resources.

You can always look for ways to cut costs, even after you've cut all you can. It is better by far to focus on selling and on doing things that make it easier to sell. Focus on creating more value, differentiating your offer from your competitors, and delivering a better customer experience.

Challenges to value-based pricing

Continuous improvement of the product and/or service

Your business needs to maintain the value the customer is getting. It must constantly strive to stay ahead of the competition. The competition is always working to improve, so you must as well. This can be achieved by constant review of the company's products and services, aiming to make them better than the competition and a better solution for more customer problems.

Organizational challenges

The marketing and sales teams need to work hand in hand to make pricing a reality. Information should be shared, especially on pricing and customer needs.

Transparency

The customer should know how the price and value have been arrived at based on the solutions provided by the business. This should be a transparent process with no surprises. Products and services should be provided after all the terms have been set, understood, and agreed upon.

Value-based pricing is beneficial to both sides of the transaction. The customer gets the best product at the best price, and the business charges a higher price because it is a great product. A business should understand customers' needs in order to customize products and services for them. This will enable the business to meet their needs far beyond their expectations.

Key Points

- The value that your solution provides is crucial to your business. Customers will pay more for a significant value.
- They will buy value and your solutions to their problems. They won't buy your *product*.
- Do your homework and know how valuable the product can be to your customer, and determine your price based on that information. This is value-based pricing.
- Show the product value in detail before giving your price offer.
- Don't focus on reducing your prices to get more sales. Put your efforts into providing your customers with what they want and need.

Chapter 15:
How to Create a Pool of B2B Sales Leads

How you sell matters much more than what you sell.

Sales leads are vital to any business. The first step to success is identifying prospective customers who might have an interest in the products and services your company offers.

There are many ways to generate sales leads, and below you will find those that I find most helpful. However, it is important for me to clarify something: learn these methods, but don't feel like you have to use all of them. Use the ones you feel most comfortable with. Just know that there are many ways to dramatically increase your sales. Be open-minded about your options, and always remember this: following up on existing hot leads is more important than spending your time looking for new ones.

In order to generate a sales lead, it is important to understand the following:

- Your product—this is vital!
- The value you provide to your customers.
- How to approach your customers and what they are looking for.

Here are some of the top ways to generate leads. The main idea is to generate *hot* sales leads.

Use referrals: People tend to trust you more if somebody introduced you or told them about you. Take advantage of the customers you already have. They can bring a lot more clients to your company. Treat them well so they will have no problem referring you to other interested firms. Also, contact your friends and former colleagues and ask if they know anyone who may be interested in your products.

Create business relations: Networking is an important aspect in generating sales leads in a B2B cycle. Meeting people is inevitable with this kind of business, so embrace it and meet as many people as possible. This will give you a diversified array of prospective clients to choose from. I would also recommend you participate in trade shows. This can go a long way toward lengthening your list of sales leads. Just pick up the contact information of the attendees who visit your tent. Meet with people, be in touch, and go to relevant events in order to create more sales leads. (See Chapter 13 for more about networking.)

Web advertising: This is gaining popularity. Most businesses attribute many of their sales leads to this tool. Creating a Web site for your firm can spread the word about you and your product. After you post an ad for the latest product you are offering, consider asking site visitors to complete a survey or a contact form. This way, you can easily contact a prospective customer.

Social media: This has become the most powerful tool for developing sales leads. It is also the cheapest form. In addition, many people visit these sites daily. Just one post describing the things you offer can attract a number of willing clients.

Partnerships: Consider entering into a sales partnership. This is a B2B sales technique that has worked for quite a few businesses. No man is an island; do not walk alone. Look for other like-minded sales experts and share sales leads with them. However, make sure they do not compete with you in any way. Work together with other sales experts with good reputations in your industry. Work with those who sell products that fit or tie in with yours, but don't compete. Having a trusting relationship with a sales partner can provide great leads and help you go after your deals.

Tele-prospecting: This is different from telemarketing, since it makes use of professionals who are either internal employees or outsourced by you. They pick calls from clients, and based on the vast knowledge they have about the product, they are able to gauge if the client is interested in the item.

Key Points

- Know the importance of generating sales leads. They are the starting point of your sales process.
- Memorize the five ways to create *hot* sales leads.
    - Use referrals
    - Create business relations
    - Web advertising
    - Social media
    - Sales partners
- Start by choosing two or three ways that you feel most comfortable with.
- Get started, and compare your results to your expectations.
- Follow up. Following up on existing hot leads is more important than spending your time looking for new leads.
- Consider using more ways than those in the above list. Think outside the box!

Chapter 16:
How to Qualify
Your Sales Leads

*Building and managing the sales pipeline
is critical to any business's success.*

N ow that you have your sales leads, you must make sure to qualify those leads. The first thing to do is decide which leads are worth your effort and which are likely to result in a dead end.

After you have gathered a database of prospective clients, the next step is to shake up the list and get to the people who are relevant to your business. Not everyone who shows a glimpse of interest in your product or service will be a longtime customer.

Learning how to properly qualify sales leads is very important, since time is a precious commodity and our target is to get a lot of sales in as little time as possible. This is especially the case in business-to-business sales, since the sales cycle can be very long. Invest your time in the leads that will bring you the most money. As you have seen, generating sales leads is an extensive and time-consuming exercise, so choose carefully.

By controlling the sales conversation and asking the right questions, you can quickly find out if you're on the right track with a potential lead. Contacting each of the leads and asking questions is a great way to assess who suits your business interests. Engage them in a conversation and make sure you are the one in control. Here are some tips you can use to qualify B2B sales leads. There are also questions you can ask during the conversation.

The first thing every salesperson, especially new ones, must understand is that *not every opportunity is worth jumping at,* and not everyone who asks for or about your offering is going to be your next big customer.

Verify that you are *talking to the right decision maker.* Make sure the person you are speaking with can make the decision and has the budget. It's okay to get the lead from someone other than the decision maker and then do some preparation before talking to the right prospect, but you must know who the right person to talk to is.

Understand what your customer needs. Know what his or her problems are and how—or if—you can solve them. This must be *for them*. Not you.

Wait on your sales pitch. Sit back and ask some probing questions to ensure you both have a good fit. Dropping your pitch too early is like turning the meeting over to the prospect, who then starts asking *you* the questions, putting you on the defensive.

They will buy from you if you can *create an emotional connection*, which you can start doing from the first meeting.

Most customers and prospects want to talk, as long as you *ask them the right questions.* When starting to talk about features and benefits, the prospect just tunes out. First, ask about their decision-making process to find out who in the company makes the purchasing calls and what the overall goals are; then ask about decision-making criteria, which helps weed out less serious prospects. Next, ask about the criteria for the vendor they're looking for, which helps determine whether it's a high-value lead.

The whole point is to ask good questions, so you take a ten-minute conversation and expand it into twenty minutes or more during your meeting. At the same time, you don't want to overwhelm the prospect with questions, because too many will turn him or her off. When you lump too many situational questions together, it becomes interrogational and can put off the potential customer. Find the right balance.

Work closely with marketing. Many tips come from the marketing and street teams, since they know tons and can verify your leads. Start qualifying your sales leads with your marketing team *before* your one-on-one meetings with your potential customers. Marketing wants to understand what the sales department is looking for, and sales has to understand the responsibilities the marketing team is facing.

Key Points

- *Create a good conversation*: Most of the time a sales prospect is someone new to you. Therefore, it is crucial to lighten the mood of the conversation. Make them feel at ease. Any careless mistake may end the discussion early. This talk should be geared toward getting to know a particular client's problems and providing the best way forward. Never start with your sales pitch. Ensure that you are both on the same page before going for the pitch.

- *Find the decision maker*: What criteria do they use to reach a decision about procurement of products? Ask about the organizational relationships that shape such decisions. This will go a long way in weeding out the duds. If you find out they have no power, find the person who does, or move on.

- *Know what they expect of you*: Ask about the criteria of the vendor they are looking for. This question will create an opportunity to put forward your values, especially when you are dealing with a high quality lead. Put everything on the table and convince them to select your firm. This is where a deep knowledge of your product comes in handy. In the B2B cycle, you are meeting with people who are very aware of what they want. If you fail to lure them with an impressive presentation of your item, be prepared to lose them.

- *Find out how urgently they need the product*: If you are hell-bent on seeing your sales rise after a short period, then a client who does not know exactly when he or she will be ordering your services should be avoided. Get to know how much time it will take them to make the first purchase.

- *Work closely with your marketing team:* You will save money and time since these people have good background information on some clients. This will reduce the number of customers you will need to meet one-on-one.

Chapter 17:
How to Follow Up
on Sales Leads

*To win sales, it's all about how you
manage and follow up your leads.*

Create sales leads.
Qualify those leads.
Now, manage your leads.

I n order to really make your sales take off, focus on how you manage your leads. Managing leads and following up with them create more sales than you can imagine.

For your business to succeed, you will need to closely monitor your sales leads regularly. Generating a pool of great customers is not adequate to keep your sales increasing. A follow up is needed once in a while.

So, how do you keep track of your sales leads? There are many applications and programs available to help follow up on your leads. Pick the one that works for you. Follow up with them the same as you follow up on every action item that crosses your desk. The difference between following up or not following up on those leads is the difference between having your next big sale or not.

These are the main action items in your follow up process.

1. *CRM*: Make sure that all sales leads are entered into your CRM (Customer Relationship Management) system as soon as they are received and that each one has immediate follow up action items. Always ensure that you record every prospective client into your CRM system. Keep track of any changes in the system.

2. *Make it a daily routine:* It is not enough to check the system only from time to time; you must check

consistently. After all, it is the only way to know that your customers are being followed up with.

3. *Be fast*: Don't get stuck in second place. Work fast. While you are waiting and not following up on your leads, your competitor is using the time to talk to the prospect. Always attend to your sales leads quickly. Never keep them waiting, or your competitors might approach them. Every time a customer poses a question relating to your product, you should be prepared to speedily provide them with accurate answers. Even a second wasted is enough for a competitor to swoop in on a sales lead. Salespeople who try to contact potential customers within an hour of receiving queries have a higher chance of getting meaningful conversations with key decision makers.

    1. *Relay quality information*: It's not just about being fast. It's also about providing quality replies. You must provide complete answers to prospective customers' questions with as little turnaround time as possible. It is not enough to be the first to respond to the customer. You must also be the first to answer their questions satisfactorily. You are looking to build a long-lasting business relationship with this client. Any time they ask questions about what your firm offers, be ready to give them nothing but the best. You must give informative answers, especially when you are dealing with top decision makers.

    2. *Improve your follow up time*: From time to time, self-check your monitoring system and note any room for improvement. Find out what your weak points are, and set some targets for your business. This gets you an overall picture of your progress.

Look into the number of leads your company gets in a week, the amount of time taken before they are responded to, and how many of those turn out to be loyal customers. If you are leaning toward the negative in any, or all, of these parameters, come up with realistic goals that will allow you to improve. The only way to improve is to keep working on it!

Follow up and provide quality responses. Build trust and credibility to dramatically increase your chances of winning the customer. The follow up process determines the number of sales a business makes within a given period of time. In a B2B cycle, if you want to stay in business for long, you need to monitor your clients.

A timely response may keep a key sales lead. If you manage your sales leads in an effective manner, you can count on a huge boost in your sales. Take it upon yourself to relay any details your leads may require about your product without hesitation. The information must be detailed and of the highest quality. Most importantly, always aim to make your potential customer trust you more. You will attract more sales with time.

Key Points

- Following up is the key to all sales activities. When there is no follow up, there is no execution.
- Monitor and manage your sales leads, using CRM and a daily routine.
- Respond to customers' questions quickly. A timely response is crucial.
- Make sure your reply has quality information about your products and good answers to their questions and requests.
- Analyze your follow up process and improve it.
- Keep following up!

Chapter 18:
B2B and Social Media

"Social media isn't something that you
'do'; instead you have to 'be' social."

—Peter Thomson, *Tickle: Digital Marketing
for Tech Companies*

S ocial media is the greatest way I have found to connect with people, especially when the goal is to meet new people in a particular industry. Selling has always revolved around relationships and networking—establishing rapport. Traditionally this has been done via face-to-face business meetings, industry conferences, social clubs, and so forth. No longer! B2B has come a long way in a short generation of sales processes, from traditional methods that utilized networking and referrals, to new approaches such as social media.

Social media is an influential platform. It allows people from all over the world to socialize and make new relationships. If you want to get to know people abroad, social media allows you to begin and maintain those relationships without the need to fly across the world. Now with social media we can get more leads, with a better success percentage, and in less time than the traditional methods—and all right from our desks.

The business world has realized the impact that social media can have in enterprise, and businesses are utilizing it to the fullest. It can be used both to gain exposure for a product and as a direct method to sell to the world. The same may be said for the business-to-business sales world. Social media has increased the scale and reach of networks, changing the way we collaborate online. Many buying decisions start through social media.

Social media enables online collaboration tools that were developed by sales organizations. Crowdsourcing is a great tool that companies have used for everything from picking potato chip flavors to building the perfect car. This is social selling. The goal is to create fundamental changes in customer *behavior* and in their *buying process*. Social media creates a new way of social selling, with new buyer behaviors. Social selling is about recognizing that the buying process is controlled by a better informed and more connected customer. Sales remains a relationship-driven business, and the new social customer demands relevance from salespeople—expecting them to know about them, their companies, and their needs before engaging. So, sales professionals are using social media to listen, engage, and add to the customer conversation. Your customer expects you to know at least as much about them as they do about you.

The Importance of Social Media

There are tons of options

Social media exposes you and your product to a wide range of people. On social media sites you will develop relationships and maintain those that are most useful to your business. Then you can start sharing information about the products and services you offer. Unlike getting contacts from a database, which limits you to only a few choices that may lack credibility, social media gives you an opportunity to seek out connections for yourself.

Affordable to anyone

Social media is very affordable compared to traditional methods. For instance, some traditional methods necessitate your traveling overseas to meet a client. If your company uses telemarketing to develop sales leads, you'll be paying huge bills every month. On social media, you can initiate a chat with a potential customer for free.

It's the fastest approach

Networking through social media enables you to give quick feedback. You can also address the concerns of many customers who have the same queries with just one message. This is impossible with any other means of selling.

Social media is flexible

You have access to your customers from anywhere with social media. With a good smartphone, you can respond to them from wherever you might be, and at home you can use your laptop to chat with your other clients and establish new business relationships without any hassles.

Interactions on social sites are becoming assets for business. You are dealing with clients who know a lot, and aren't afraid to shop around. Always keep in mind that they have the means and the connections to get what they want. Therefore, it is very important that you customize every conversation to suit their individual needs. They may tolerate your scanty knowledge about them, since you are meeting for the very first time, but then again, they may not. Don't take the risk.

Getting to know your potential customers is easy now, with Web sites like LinkedIn and the Internet in general. Make sure you know them, even a little. Then you can start convincing them that your product will solve their problems. To do successful business through social media, you have to be on the ball.

Key Points

- Understand the importance of social media and how it can influence your business.
  - Variety of options and tools
  - Affordable to anyone
  - Fastest approach
  - Flexible
- Know the effects of *not* using social media and sticking with traditional methods.
- Know the impact and the importance of social selling. Social media creates fundamental changes in customer behavior and the buying process.
- Use social media to get to know more about your customers and what they are looking for. Use this great platform to connect and share important information with them.
- Use social media to help you reach out to new customers and new markets.
- Use social media to learn about potential customers before you sell to them. This is in addition to listening and engaging in the customer conversation.
- Take advantage of the many benefits of social media. Think about advertising products, and utilize tools like affordable communication, such as chatting. Provide instant feedback to many customers at once and from the comfort of your office or home.
- Be out there, in the right way. Be positive, useful, and insightful.

Chapter 19:
How to Generate
B2B Sales With
Social Media

"We don't have a choice on whether we do social
media. The question is how well we do it."

–Erik Qualman

S ocial media can give a boost to your sales if managed properly. With all the benefits outlined above, we will only be seeing more businesses shifting to this option. As discussed earlier, social media is a great way to attract more customers. Here, you will make good long-lasting relationships from a simple conversation. However, I would also recommend you integrate it with other methods, because of course you want to actually *know* the people you will be doing business with.

Keep in mind that even in this digital, Internet-driven age, the personal touch still matters. Social media is the place for first contact and maintaining existing relationships, but there is nothing that can replace a face-to-face meeting. Maybe it's just human nature to want to see the person you're giving money to, to know the person who can help you, or to see that there is a face to the service—and an actual person behind the profile. Whatever the reason, don't forget to show your humanity. Use social media, but don't rely on it solely to boost your sales.

Generating sales with social media

Stay connected: In order to build your social network, you must start one. First, establish a site that will attract your targeted clients. Second, create profiles on a few sites that are capable of selling your business. Don't be too informal, as this may deter some of the more serious potential customers.

Be on the lookout for great opportunities: People on social media talk about things that interest them. Listen to what people are talking about, and look for the right opportunities to jump on for your business. An idea could come from the most unlikely source.

Stay actively involved: Being on social media is one thing, but being influential is quite another. For companies, quantity matters. For instance, the number of fans you have appears to correlate to the number of customers you have. Engage them in meaningful conversations, and get to know their specific needs by asking the necessary questions. Ask anything you don't know their answer to. Asking the right questions and starting discussions in the right forums is a great way to align your thoughts with other people's needs. The customer's thoughts and needs are what drive the market. Constant involvement in social media gives you the power to know where you are compared to the world, and gives you the opportunity and ability to influence other people's thoughts.

Stay positive: With a single post containing an image of your product online, you can get thousands of views. Some viewers will comment, and some comments might be negative. It is your responsibility to welcome all opinions and reply in a positive manner. Use the criticism to your advantage. Is there really something to be improved? Does that person not know what he's talking about? Always post a positive reply, thanking them for their comment. Show that you are using the comments to improve, and always stay classy.

Give inspiring information: Using social media lets you inspire other people by providing them with new and interesting information.

Be responsive: It's extremely important to reply to social media e-mails and messages. Treat them like an e-mail or call from a prospective customer. Be prompt, attentive, and courteous.

Be honest: It's totally acceptable to say, "I don't know, but let me find out for you," or to give a flat-out *no*. These replies are indicative of your honesty and are evidence that you are a real person and not some sort of sales cyborg. Under-promise and over-deliver. It's a cliché for a reason. Exceeding client expectations is the only acceptable result, and client and customer alike will appreciate your honesty.

Stand for Value: Always convey and represent your business values and goals in your interactions. This is commonly known as social selling—and social selling comes before social media. This includes everything from having honorable business practices to having the highest quality product. If you use YouTube or Twitter, consider featuring your business values or goals in a post.

Stand out from the crowd: It is on you to create and portray unique qualities that will attract customers to you and not to the competition.

Educate your clients: You are in control here, so give your customers some essential information on how to use your products in efficient ways that will aid their business. Consider including ways of using the product they might not have thought of. Opening options to your customers through education is a great way to retain and expand your customer base.

Create new connections for them: Connecting your client with potential customers and vendors of their own is a great way to improve your team member status. This helps improve your sales, since those clients will refer you to other people as well. Be a valuable member of someone else's network. It will help them *and* you.

Involve your customers: Your clients want to be involved in your business, and it is important for them that you are successful. They have made an investment in you and your company. Engage with them when you are making key decisions about your company. For instance, collect their feedback on what you offer. In addition, get their views on what they would like to be included in the next new product.

Help them find new opportunities: Now that you are fully established on social media, look for new openings for your clients. These can be achieved using free search tools such as Google Alerts or Social Mention.

Key Points

- Make sure you stay connected using social media, and create a good profile that can sell your business.
- Look out for great opportunities and leads. Stay tuned and you will get more opportunities.
- Be actively involved. Engage and be influential on social media by having meaningful conversations and asking questions.
- Respond to the opinions directed at you, whether positive or negative. Replying to other people is very important on social media.
- Give inspiring information. Inspire your audience, and make them want your opinion.
- Be honest with your clients, especially in regard to what you can deliver.
- Stand for value by representing your business values to your customers.
- Use social media to educate your clients about your products and connect them to others who can use their services.
- Be a useful member of other people's networks. Create new and important connections for other people in your network.
- Involve your customers. Ask them for their opinion, and give them the opportunity to influence and be a part of your decision.

Chapter 20:
How to Sell Anything to Anyone

*With the right sales structure, we can sell anything
to anyone, from a product to thoughts and ideas.*

B eing in sales not only means selling your products but also selling your ideas to your boss, and selling your skills and abilities to a potential employer. Your success will depend on your ability to close a sale. Not everyone was born to be a salesperson, but you can learn and become an expert easily. Sales is all about connecting with other people and having them see things from your point of view. If you can manage to get them on board and see your point, negation and closing the deal is the easiest thing to do.

There are four critical concepts to learn how to sell anything to anyone. Once you learn these concepts, practice them on a daily basis and customize them to your situation.

1. Do your homework so you can understand your customer or anyone else you intend to sell to. Know about their roles and objectives. On the same note, have a comprehensive understanding and knowledge of your offering, whether it is a product, a plan, or an idea. Clear up any doubts you might have before you approach your audience. If the boss or customer outwits you, you will not get anything from your efforts and you will have wasted everyone's time.

2. Learn to ask and listen. You have done your homework and completely understand the product, but you should also know how to present your ideas to your audience. The wrong presentation comes across as pushy. Learning to ask and listen will help you understand the needs of the people you are selling to and how the product can

help them achieve their goals. Listening will help you know what matters to your customers and will help you determine how to present the product or idea in a way that they will see its benefits rather than disadvantages.

3. Strive to form a deep, genuine relationship—a meaningful connection—between you and your customer. To achieve this, you will need to explain things in a way they understand. This relationship can tell you what an individual is looking for and how to address his or her concerns appropriately.

4. Know which side you are on. It is essential that you always keep in mind that you are working for the *customer* and trying to sell the product or item to them as a way of helping them meet their goals. Selling is all about convincing your customer of your ability to make them more successful than they are and proving it to them.

Key Points

- Anyone can learn how to sell and how to boom sales using these main points.
  - Start by understanding your customer and knowing the product you intend to sell.
  - Learn how to present your ideas to your audience. Using the right words and the right story can help you sell anything to anyone.
  - Learn how to ask questions and listen to the answers.
  - Explain things clearly and specifically to your customers. Understand what they are looking for in a product.
  - Understand that you are selling the product to help them meet their goals.

Chapter 21:
How to Handle
Fears in Sales

"Do what you fear most and you control fear."

—Tom Hopkins

F ear of public speaking, fear of customer interaction, fear of taking chances, and fear of grabbing opportunities. These all boil down to one real fear: fear of rejection and failure. Imagine being completely prepared, with extensive product knowledge and good marketing strategy, and not even getting a nod from the customers after your presentation. This frustrating possibility is the reason most salespeople go for the certainty of a done deal. They do not approach every customer who comes their way. Instead, they cater to those they consider the best potential customers.

This belief and behavior must disappear. Instead of clinging to negative perceptions, there must be a change in outlook. First, accept that anything can happen in the field. There may be *yes* and *no* answers from the clients. If it's a *yes*, that's great! If it's a *no*—well, it's great that you tried. When sales don't come through, create new opportunities—opportunities to learn, to find new things, and to be inspired. Just because you fail once doesn't mean you are a failure. All those who succeed had their own taste of failure before they made it to the big time.

Another way to deal with your sales fear is to understand the customer's perspective. If the answer is *no*, it probably doesn't mean the customer didn't like *you*. The customer may just be saying *no* for now, and there is a possibility of a *yes* in the future. If this is the case, then you need to build a strong relationship so that possibility will become a reality. Take a look at your approach, too. If you're intimidating the customer, then you are most likely not going to make the sale. Remember that selling is also serving. You are selling to serve the needs of the customer.

Make sure that you focus on what they really need, and never overwhelm them with your extensive product knowledge.

The fact is that we are living in a negative world. We are led to believe that we need this, that, and the other in order to be safe. Rather than focusing on the positive, we focus on the negative. The good thing is we can counteract all of this. It's just a matter of having the proper perspective on life.

Counteracting Fear

When it comes to sales, accept that there will be roadblocks in the way: competitors, fear of facing customers, imperfect skills, and more. Rather than focusing on those, think of ways to counteract them. Do you have too many competitors? Highlight the best selling point of your product that your competitors don't have. Do you have a fear of public speaking or approaching a customer? Be convinced that you'll get a *yes*, and if not, just say there are others waiting. Don't know the product? Study and research it. In every fear or roadblock, there is a corresponding solution. Focus on the solution and not on the problem.

Key Points

- Don't be afraid. It's only sales!
- Do not fear rejection in making sales. If you get a *yes*, that's great! If you get a *no*, move on and learn from it. Learn from the *no* and create new opportunities.
- Understand the customer's perspective and why he or she has declined to buy. Create a relationship for a future *yes*.
- Enjoy it! Sales is fun!

Chapter 22:
How to Create
Loyal Customers

*Customer service is a priority across
all units of the business.*

C ongratulations! You made the sale! Now comes a whole new challenge. Keep that customer loyal to you and to your company. In B2B, there are many ways to achieve customer loyalty. The most vital is the way you handle your customers—customer service.

Customer service is paramount to any business today. As opposed to the traditional setting where customer service was separate from sales, today customer service is across all units of the business, not just sales and support. Customer service in B2B includes how—and how quickly—you reply to your customer. But replying is not all. It's important how quickly you provide a *professional* reply, and how efficiently and professionally you close the customer service cycle. It sounds easy to accomplish, right? Making customers happy is a constant job that includes all the divisions of the company. If you create more customers and are able to retain them, more revenue comes into your company, and everyone thrives.

These days, there aren't huge differences between the products available in the market. The differences between one solution and another get smaller every day, and sometimes they are only one version apart. In most cases, the difference between your product and your competitor's product isn't huge. One of the ways to make your offering more attractive can be—and should be—your customer support.

Great customer service is a very effective way to make your company special and different from all the others in the market. This includes the way you treat your customers and the way you make them feel. An emotional response to the product is the best thing you can give your customers, and it also creates brand loyalty. As Dr. Thomas L. Garthwaite said, "People may not remember exactly what you did, or what you said, but they will always remember how you made them feel."

Good customer service means that your customers will know that no matter what, you are there for them. This comes down to three vital *how-tos.*

1. Build a trusting relationship: One thing that will bring your customers back again and again is your customer service. That includes your honesty and gaining their trust. Good customer service will make your customer trust you and believe in you.

2. Understand your customer's needs: It is important that the customer know that you understand what he or she wants and really needs. Understanding the customer is crucial to great customer service.

3. Be available and kind: Your customers must know that you are there for them when they need you. But it's not enough to be there; you must be kind and responsive as well.

Great customer service is a methodology, and it must permeate every level and division of a company. It's a way of running the company. Although customer service is the best way to create customer loyalty, it is just part of the bigger picture of business and brand success. Many other factors help create loyal customers, but this is the place to start. Improve your customer service, and set your company apart.

Key Points

- Keep your customers coming to you over and over.
- Customer service is important to maintaining customers.
- Customer service functions across all units of your organization. Provide the best customer service in all the departments of the business, and by all employees.
- Give a professional reply to your customers as quickly as possible.
- Build a trusting relationship with your customers. Understand their needs and always be available to them.

"It is not enough to do your best. You need to know what to do and then do your best."

—Edward Deming

www.ingramcontent.com/pod-product-compliance
Lightning Source LLC
Chambersburg PA
CBHW022002170526
45157CB00003B/1105